Come in at Random
in any Key you like

Sue Thompson

Come in at Random
in any Key you like

ISBN: 978-1986478472

British Library Cataloguing in Publication Data.
A CIP catalogue record for this book is available from the British Library.

DEDICATION

To all those hard working musicians out there who bring so much joy to our lives

Thanks and Acknowledgments

It has been a great joy for me to write this book as I have had for the last year a perfect excuse to travel the leafy lanes of Suffolk drinking beer, eating pies and listening to music.

New friendships have been formed and I now find myself welcomed by musicians who put up with me lurking in corners scribbling notes about them, so I would like to thank the following people for encouraging me and making this book possible:

To Mark and Marie of the White Horse for madness, mayhem and the world's best pies. Also for their permission to use the pic of the pub on my front cover.

David of the Froize, a tireless supporter of music and provider of legendary food.

Chris and Carrie from the Sorrel Horse.

Susie Hammond and everyone connected with the Blaxhall Ship music nights.

Horse Clarke and all his friends for the
Wednesday evening fun and frolics.

Doris the Singing Barmaid, sorry we let you down
with our performance but at least we tried!

Mat Bayfield for always being such an inspiration
and so much fun.

The Colombines for providing me with a great
idea for the title of this book and also for giving
me permission to reproduce the words to their
song 'Silver Gilt Strings'.

Lucy and John aka Honey and the Bear, Kevin
and Kelly who are always worth watching, and the
amazing Burkitt family, I'm sure you'll all be
famous one day.

Thank you all, keep on doing what you do and
watch out for the strange lady with the notebook,
she'll be watching you.

And last but not least: to Suzan Collins for her
support and direction.

Contents

A Surprise Party

You could say without fear of contradiction that the area we have chosen for our home in East Suffolk is remote. It is also quiet. Large crowds of people are rare, unless you can count crowds of birdwatchers who arrive en masse at the merest rumour of the sighting of a rare bird to be captured on film.

They're all the same to me, birds, boring brown things that go tweet, but I digress.

Noisy crowds in our part of the world are as rare as windless days on Shingle Street, so the night of the Great Real Ale Enthusiasts Invasion of the Swan at Alderton was a night to remember.

It was the evening of 10th March 2017, a quiet Thursday night in the dark depths of the Suffolk countryside, the only lights in the little village peeping from the leaded windows of the cosy pub. A small, discreet band of music lovers were huddled round the bar to support our good friend Kevin Sullivan in his brave attempt to start up an open mic evening at the Swan.

It's not an easy task to get musicians from more populous areas of Suffolk such as Snape and Aldeburgh to come to the 'back of beyond' as we tend to be called by such townies. So often it is just Kevin and his trusty guitar. Kevin likes to pay tribute to recently deceased famous musicians, so you can image how he enjoyed the grim harvest of 2016. Bowie, Prince, George Michael, Leonard Cohen, their best-known songs would be reverently performed for our enjoyment. Kevin certainly had plenty of material to choose from.

Around a dozen of us had gathered in the bar and settled down for a gentle evenings' entertainment when the door suddenly burst open and the carnival began. Around twenty seven people (it felt like many more, believe me) bounded into the Swan, all talking at once, loudly. I think they may have been drinking.

It transpired that we had been singled out by a party of real ale enthusiasts on a coach trip from Ipswich, who were taking a guided pub crawl around the isolated hostelries of the Bawdsey Peninsula. I think that we were pub number three.

The enthusiasts (great name for a band, by the way) came in all shapes and sizes and both sexes, somehow resembling a gathering of life-sized garden gnomes.

As crews go, they couldn't have been motley-er, some being quite startlingly well-built and others more your dwarf variety. One sported a fetching afro hairstyle which scraped the low beamed ceiling of the Swan. I think he may have also been wearing a tank top, reminiscent of the disco dancing days of the '70s. This bunch was raucous, rowdy and totally wonderful. We had a party on our hands.

The enthusiasts turned out to be great minglers. It felt as if we had known them since our own disco dancing days, and the sound of our merry-making bounced off the old pub walls for around an hour until suddenly they just took off, like a flock of birds startled by a predator.

I think the coach driver had reminded them that there was still one more quiet country pub for them to enliven before closing time so putting an end to their shenanigans. We waved them off like family at Christmas with cries of 'Safe journey' and 'Be sure to come back soon'. And then they were gone, leaving a ringing in the ears and a waft of real ale on the air.

Kevin reached for his guitar once more and began to sing, quietly and with much reverence 'Ground control to Major Tom…'

The White Horse, Sweffling

When Pete and I got married in the summer of 1970, we didn't buy any of our own furniture. No trips to John Lewis, or even Ikea, for us. Instead, all our items were donated by our parents, grateful to get rid of stuff they didn't want and had been trying to offload for years, or even more grateful friends who were moving on from items they had inherited from their own parents and just couldn't live with anymore.

Our first home, an unlovely rented flat at the top of a run-down house in a very seedy area near the Kursaal in Southend, was furnished with these battered remnants of other people's lives. We didn't care, we were playing house for real. Aged twenty, poverty-stricken but quite sickeningly loved-up, we would have happily lived in a tent if it meant living in it together.

I had forgotten just how happy we had been with our cast-offs until one cold and windy January day, after a long tiring charity walk, Pete and I stumbled into the fairyland that is the White Horse in Sweffling.

It was all there, the high chairs doubling up as bar stools, the comfy sofas that had probably been doing the rounds since the '70s (perhaps we had once owned some of them ourselves), the mis-matched, misshapen oddments of our youth re-discovered in a forgotten corner of Suffolk. Even Trusty Trudie, our long suffering satnav, struggles to find Sweffling.

Many people think it's not a place but a rude pastime for country folk such as ourselves.

Pete and I relaxed into a corner seat, bought a pie and a beer each, and were suddenly twenty years old again. You can't keep us away from the White Horse now. We keep finding excuses to go back. Sweffling is eighteen and a half miles away from our home in Hollesley, and believe me it feels much further, but it's well worth the effort to get there.

Our first revisit was, as is far too often the case with ourselves and pubs, food related. In this case, for the White Horse Authentic Curry Night. We had discovered the talents of the chef, Nick Lingard, on our Shingle Street charity walk back in January.

It became the highlight of the walk when we discovered the intriguing paper bags Nick was carrying contained home-made onion bhajis. I managed to snaffle a few, well quite a few, on the way round to ward off the icy blasts roaring in from the North Sea.

When I discovered that Nick travelled the curry-starved regions of Suffolk bringing spicy delights to his legions of fans, I made a mental note to travel any distance to share the bounty. It is Nick's mission to light up the lives of hungry curry lovers in far-flung locations such as Butley, Boyton and of course Sweffling - spreading joy and increased waistlines among the deprived hordes.

He turned up at the White Horse bringing his giant pots of magic with him. There was a choice of curry, goat or veggie, the famous bhajis and Nick had also brought along enough rice to feed the whole of Suffolk.

Around fifty of us had pre-booked as Nick is famous in these parts and news of his feasts travels fast. We squeezed into the back room of the White Horse clutching our plates and cutlery in eager anticipation.

Nick hoisted the huge pots onto the range, removed the lids and began to stir. All eyes were glued to the steaming contents. The temperature in the tiny room rose to sauna-like levels, some brave souls even removed their coats and scarves. And then the smell hit - it was all we could do not to mob Nick in our eagerness to tuck in.

Soon all were served and a blissful silence descended. Belts were loosened, buttons undone and at last we sat back in our comfy chairs, replete and sleepy. We needed beer, and we had come to the right place.

The White Horse keeps a range of East Anglian beers, served by gravity straight from the cask. They have won prizes for it.

However, you will search in vain for a bar. Instead the busy owners, Marie and Mark, are constantly running in and out of the tap room to keep their customers satisfied. They make their own non-alcoholic drinks too, among them my own favourite which is called a nojito.

I don't know what they put in it. Mint seems to feature strongly amongst the ingredients giving it a fresh healthy taste and it is the only soft drink I have found in a pub so far that I actually like. Believe me I've been looking for a long, long time.

Another reason to visit Sweffling, apart from the thrill of the journey, which sometimes feels like the opening scene from *An American Werewolf in London*, is the cinema night, imaginatively known as Swefflix.

This is the White Horse's own Cinema Paradiso, and takes place in the lounge area, into which so much seating has been crammed you can barely stand up again once seated.

The projector is balanced on a coat stand. The screen is about four feet by three feet, and the film flickers like a silent movie.

That evening we went to see *Withnail and I*. You could not get a more perfect setting to see this film, which is up there with *Local Hero* and *The Rocky Horror Picture Show* as one of my all-time favourite movies.

We each took along our own snacks, which seemed to consist largely of packets of crisps and other sundry salty health foods, and one of the White Horse regulars had kindly provided trays of sausage and tatty combos, nicely themed to the film, so that we wouldn't go hungry, or to tempt us to buy beer. Not that we needed any encouragement to do that.

Free glasses of sherry were provided in the first interval. It was a long time since I had tried sherry. *I*t was a lot nicer than I expected and also an appropriate accompaniment to the film.

Another delightful feature of Swefflix is the random interval alarm. This consists of an old alarm clock which is set to activate when it is deemed the audience may be in need of refreshment (of course they are!) and a queue swiftly forms outside the tap room. Jugs of ale and bowls of salty snacks are passed out and the audience resume their seats. I counted at least three of these breaks. It does wonders for the mood of the filmgoers and the profits of the pub, a real win/win combination.

As the evening progressed and the film-goers mellowed nicely, it became an audience-participation free for all. A few people seemed to be able to quote the whole film, while others would join in with a haphazard line when it came back to them. The 'Camberwell Carrot' episode proved particularly popular, I recall.

We finally emerged into the thick blackness of the Sweffling night at around 11pm, having hoovered up the last of the crisps and any remaining tatties, and began the perilous journey through the unlit country lanes to the safety of the A12 and home. This time Trudie didn't let us down.

When I started research for this book, I didn't expect to rediscover my musical youth in the process, but this has now happened thanks to Mark and Marie's Old School Blowout, which is held in the pub every third Wednesday evening.

The event is stage managed by the charismatic Horse Clarke and consists of some old-fashioned DJ-ing (bring your own vinyl if you wish or just broaden your horizons and see what Horse has to offer. You know it'll be good) and then at around 9pm, when everyone is sufficiently lubricated and relaxed, the real fun can begin.

The White Horse is the nearest thing a pub can get to also being a music shop. Walls and shelves hold a treasury of instruments from ukuleles to sitars with percussion instruments (my own particular favourites) laid out on the tables for those of us whose skills add up to being able to bash a tambourine in time to the music.

It's good to feel included, and not being expected to sing is a big bonus too.

Pete, however, is in ukulele heaven. He wanders around the pub lovingly picking up instruments at random and attempting to tune them in. Some are beyond help, but this doesn't stop him trying.

Someone should offer him this post as a permanent job, an out of tune ukulele is only really good for firewood. Some unkind people think this fate should also apply to *ukes that are in tune.

*Uke is the common short form of 'Ukulele'.

Pete brings with him to the Sweffling blowout nights a small rucksack into which he has packed his harmonica collection (he has eight and is threatening to buy more...) and his much-loved kazoo.

This is very popular with the Wednesday night crowd, who now demand a kazoo solo as part of their evening's entertainment.

This can be a bit risky for the kazoo player because if you don't really know a song and are just kazoo-ing along with the flow it can be terrifying if everyone stops singing and looks expectantly at you.

The ensuing silence can seem to go on forever.

One of the reasons I love percussion instruments so much is that no-one would ever ask for a tambourine solo and therefore I can safely lurk in corners with my beer and bash away undisturbed.

It is the perfect instrument for the talentless person who still wants to feel part of the scene. I can even pretend to be Stevie Nicks from Fleetwood Mac, a favourite occupation of mine when I think no-one is looking.

Although I don't recall her banging a tambourine in time to Black Magic

Woman or Go Your Own Way, it would have been fun to watch.

Personally, I feel that Fleetwood Mac were a bit full of themselves, as were many of the early bands.

You'd have thought with all the booze flying around they could have managed to be a bit more cheerful about life, but perhaps back then it wasn't cool to be seen to be having fun.

Come to think of it, things haven't changed much since then. Look at Radiohead, if ever a band needed happy pills… You could make a game out of this: match the percussion instrument to the artist - Patti Smith on the xylophone, Coldplay on rattles, Rhianna on triangle (that woman needs to lighten up), or how about Jay Z on fiddlesticks, I'd pay to see that - but not very much.

My love for percussion instruments dates back to my distant schooldays before someone decided that all children had a talent and it had to be uncovered at all costs.

Back then it was okay to admit that the best option for some children was to give them a stick and a saucepan and leave them to it.

I have a precious photograph of my schoolgirl self, aged around seven, dressed incongruously as a chicken for my part in the school nativity play. My costume consisted of a laminated picture of a chicken which hung around my neck, and my school uniform. Worked for me.

In the picture there is an expression of deep concentration on my face, my moment to shine was coming. Clutched in those small, trembling fingers is a large triangle, and you can tell by the way I am pursing my lips and screwing up my eyes that I am COUNTING...

I had probably been counting from the moment of stepping onto the stage, wouldn't want to 'ting' in the wrong place now would I? They may not ask me again.

I used to think I could sing, going as far as joining our local church choir when I was around twelve, although a large part of the reason behind this uncharacteristic brush with holiness was the fact that we got paid for singing at weddings and funerals.

When I look back now, this strikes me as bizarre. What kind of person would want a bunch of random children singing hymns at their relative's funeral?

It didn't help that we found it hard to keep a straight face on these solemn occasions - there is something about knowing that you **mustn't** laugh that just has that effect on twelve-year olds. You look around at the sad little faces and then you see someone's lip turn up and that's enough to get the giggles started.

Before you know it, there are twenty small people coughing and gasping with the effort to stop joining in with this inappropriate merriment. Faces turn red, eyes water and the occasional snort is heard.

Weddings were even worse. What was it about the Wedding March that had us in stitches? Was it the desire to substitute alternative words, some of them really quite rude, that had us reaching for the hankies and burying our heads in our song sheets? Or the sight of all those ridiculous hats on the ladies or comb-over attempts by the men, or the antics of those oh-so-cute bridesmaids and pageboys when they thought no-one was looking.

Such innocent fun and we got five bob apiece too. No wonder there was a growing list to join the choir.

My days as a chorister sadly came to an end when it came to light that my parents had neglected to have me christened. I therefore didn't fulfil the requirements needed by a member of St Lawrence Church Choir to prove that I was holy enough to sing 'Love Divine, all Loves Excelling' or 'Abide With Me' as the occasion demanded. Their loss.

But enough about me and my strange past and one final tale from the White Horse.

Just when you think their own brand of malarkey can't get any weirder, along comes Griff Pilchard. This night's entertainment was promoted on Facebook as a 'very silly act', so you couldn't say that we hadn't been warned, but even so nothing could have prepared us for Griff.

He turned out to be a lovely, friendly guy, quiet and sensible, nothing really of the Monty Python about him at all. Until, that is, he gets up to perform. The transformation is spectacular then as Griff's inspired madness is unleashed. Audience participation is mandatory, no shrinking violets allowed. Griff will find you and point you out. There are no exceptions to the rule, we'll all make merry fools of ourselves tonight.

First up is the 'Parrot Song' (no, not THAT one, this Parrot is alive and kicking!). But it could be endangered…

The audience participation consisted of repeating key words at the tops of our voices.

I'm not sure why it was so funny and I didn't even have the excuse of alcoholic consumption as that night I was on the nojitos.

So, altogether now…
Griff: 'Some people have got a parrot'
Audience, at the tops of their voices:
'PARROT!'
Griff, in a normal voice, as if any of this made sense:
'I 'ave got an 'ammer.'

Audience (we've got the hang of this by now):
'AMMER!'
Repeat several times.
'And I bash nails in with it!'

The gist of the song seemed to be that while bashing nails in with a hammer is acceptable, bashing nails in with a parrot can be rather messy.

I am so glad that Griff is around to enlighten us potential handy-persons. They should have put him on the TV with Barry Bucknell. It would have livened up the programme no end and given it a bit of class.

Moving on from Parrots, we now encounter Wally the Wasp.
Griff (perched perilously on his bar stool, brimming pint in hand),
'Who's that buzzing in my ear? It's

Wally'

Audience, volume as before,

'WALLY THE WASP!

Griff (waving his pint mug and rocking the bar stool on one leg):

'Who's that swimming in my beer? It's Wally.'

Audience:

'WALLY THE WASP!'

Then we all peer nervously into our Wally-less glasses and realise it's time for a refill.

I think Sweffling should qualify for the Suffolk Village of Culture award on this performance alone, who needs Shakespeare?

There are songs about farting (the audience are encouraged to blow raspberries at random). Reluctant refusers are embarrassed into joining in by the rest of us who stare at them in silence until a raspberry is produced. When it comes to audience participation in the White Horse, it can definitely get a bit "Lord of the Flies". Those shy souls of a nervous disposition should perhaps choose a quieter pub. Or stronger beer.

Griff's finale is perhaps the most terrifying thing I have witnessed at a music night. He tilts his stool at an impossible angle, squats on it like a chameleon waiting to pounce, and begins to creak...

'Eeeeeeeiiiiieeeiiiiiiiiiiiiiiiiieeeeeeeeeee!'

This sound goes on for so long that newcomers to the Griff Pilchard experience can become a little concerned for his welfare, but it is all part of the act.

'Eeeeeeeeiiiiieeeiiiiiiiiiiiiiiiiieeeeeeeeeee!'
I LOVE A WEE DRAM!!!!'

At this point Griff topples from the stool, takes a swig from his beer, balances back in the chameleon position and recommences his tale.

The problem was that whenever we thought Griff had finished, he would start again and his 'Eeiiiiiiiiiiiiiii' would become so alarming we would find ourselves scanning the walls for a defibrillator. Or looking anxiously around the room for a sober paramedic (fat chance). Or perhaps a wee dram.

Mark and Marie seemed to be having a bumper evening at the tap room, well, all this audience participation is thirsty work.

Hunting the Talent

Our good friend and musical impresario, Chris from the Sorrel Horse, sometimes attaches the words to the songs he intends performing to his guitar, a fine example of professional forethought if ever there was one.

I can't help wishing that other performers would follow his lead, it would save their audiences much head-scratching and sore throats.

At some time during a gig, one of the performers usually pipes up with something along the lines of 'If you know the all words you are welcome to help me out here'.

Well of course we don't know all the words, you daft lazy moronic excuse for a troubadour, that's why we've dragged ourselves to the back of beyond to hear you sing them for us. In the right order. If you can manage to play in tune. If it's not too much trouble!

But, of course, the temptation to join in is too hard to resist for long and this is where that famous Suffolk creativity springs into action.

We may not know all the words, but that doesn't stop us making them up as we go along or even deliberately singing the words to other songs, just for the hell of it.

It's like a musical version of 'Chinese Whispers', sometimes with a few rude words thrown in too from the more beer-friendly end of the room, otherwise known as the bar. Sometimes the singer even gives up and leaves us to it and then we stutter to a halt and look at each other blankly as if to say, 'What are we all doing here?'

Then there are the songs that the musicians have written themselves, like Doris, the Singing Barmaid. Doris has become one of my favourite characters from the magical musical carousel that is the Suffolk folk scene.

She is German. She is blonde, and very, very happy and grateful to be here. She writes incredibly sad songs about tragic events in foreign lands which she sings with all the cheerfulness and bonhomie of a Chas and Dave recital.

We try not to look as if we are enjoying ourselves too much as we don't want to offend her, but Doris is so happy to be here that she smiles through her desperate songs before putting down her guitar and clearing our tables on her way back to her duties behind the bar.

One eager punter was heard to ask on one occasion if he could get a beer as Doris was tuning up and her dead-pan reply was 'You won't get served, I'm out here'.

This raises the interesting concept that not only can the audience come to the rescue of those singers who have forgotten their words but we can help ourselves at the bar too. Community spirit at its best.

Brave Doris dedicates her songs to 'The friends who are no longer with me', and although I would love to know the stories behind these songs I cannot bring myself to ask her.

The last time I heard Doris perform she announced that her new song was written to celebrate being saved by Suffolk and how she was now ready to fall in love again.

Well, as you can imagine the audience put down their glasses, stopped whatever they were doing and called out, 'Who is it, Doris, TELL US NOW!' but Doris came over all coy and started clearing tables, although she hinted that she would keep us updated on the romance front in case we needed to rush out and buy hats.

Towards the end of one memorable Blaxhall Busk night, I remember we were all sitting back comfortably eating chips and chatting during a musical break when Susie, who organises the evenings, called out 'Anyone performing?'

A dazed looking old hippie called John, who seemed to have woken up from a deep sleep sometime during Woodstock, attempted to introduce himself by saying, 'Some of you may have seen me before…', pregnant pause '…then you can tell the others'.

There followed a puzzled silence. I don't think any of us had seen him before. I'm sure we would have remembered if we had and I can't recall what he sang either but it was certainly mellow. Perhaps he was an old friend of Donovan.

Later on, he came out with my favourite Blaxhall Busk quote of all time when someone asked what we, the long-suffering fans, would like a little more of and his rejoinder was 'talent'. As one of the musicians at the Butley Oyster remarked recently 'mediocrity will not be tolerated'.

Then the final act took to the stage. He slipped in quietly, almost as an afterthought.

He had a look of the Indian brave about him, as if his name should have been 'Stormy Wind on the Prairie' or 'Big Chief Little Guitar'.

He started in great style with Bob Marley's 'Redemption Song'. Honestly, I love 'Redemption Song'. It makes me want to hold up a lighted candle and cry.

I managed to resist though. I don't think this kind of behaviour would go down too well at the Blaxhall Busk where they prefer a more hi-di-hi attitude towards communal singing - you can sway but you can't sob.

He followed this with 'No Woman, No Cry' and I was so blissed out by now that I managed to order myself a glass of Merlot instead of the slimline tonic I'd promised myself for my holiday diet.

Never mind, it's a well-known fact that there are no calories present on Blaxhall Busk nights. Even in the chips.

One of the many joys of travelling around the pubs and folk venues of Suffolk is meeting the varied and fascinating characters who appear on the circuit. We often give them amusing nicknames, largely because we have forgotten their real names or feel that the prosaic and everyday titles given to our heroes by their parents are somehow inadequate for the larger than life personalities they belong to.

We recently met a talented base guitarist from Sevenoaks who had travelled down to the Blaxhall Ship with his wife and taken up residence in their camper van in the car-park. Now there's dedication for you.

His given name is Alan but our master of ceremonies at The Ship, Roger, took to calling him Dave (perhaps Roger is a fan of 'Only Fools & Horses').

So being a quick witted and inventive bunch, our table took to calling him Dave Allen, after the late lamented Irish comedian. We started making Dave Allen type gestures too, pretending to sip at whisky glasses and puffing on invisible cigarettes.

Alan/Dave looked confused, perhaps he isn't a fan. Or perhaps he didn't drive down from Sevenoaks in a camper van to be mocked by idiots in the Blaxhall Ship. Still, he played a mean bass guitar.

On June 8th, election night, which we were trying to avoid at all costs, we rocked up to the Busk to find that apart from the usual table of suspects in our corner the only people present were the musicians.

This made for a very different mood, we felt that anything could happen, that we had created our own little world where Jeremy and Theresa didn't exist (how I wish it were that easy). Even Doris seemed emboldened, entering into the spirit of things by making Donald Trump jokes.

The highlight of the evening for me, however, was when an intriguing guy introduced only as JJ proceeded to sing his own composition, a song he wrote in celebration of his divorce.

He began by explaining that he writes his own songs so that people can't tell him he's got them wrong. Don't think that will stop us JJ. Wait till you try singing it again and we'll be there to correct you if you make a mistake.

He went on to recount how his divorce song had won a competition for most miserable song of the year.

This got us very excited, misery is our thing in Blaxhall. We craned forward in eager anticipation and we weren't to be disappointed.

JJ's song even had a doleful chorus for us to sing along with, and this was no hardship as the chorus was, 'And the vultures screamed, 'It's time to Rock and Roll'.

We all got rather carried away with the spirit of this song and were sorry when it came to an end so we called out for more but I think JJ had had enough of us by then and slunk off to visit Doris at the bar.

Silver Gilt Strings

In 2013, an Arts Festival was held in Harwich at which one of the installations was a piano placed on the beach in a position where it would eventually be carried away by the tide. Members of the public were invited to play and a duet was specially written for the occasion.

The installation was called 'Eastern Exposure Piano Transplant number four', which makes me wonder what happened to the other three. Did they float away with the tide and end up on the beaches of Felixstowe? The duet itself was entitled 'Fanfare for Piano, Sea and Sky' which I think is rather poetic and charming.

I mention this story as it has been made into a haunting song by a folk group consisting of three ladies called the Colombines.

Pete and I came across them one night at the Sorrel Horse when another band we had been looking forward to seeing cancelled at the last minute. We were disappointed but decided to go along anyway to see what the Colombines would offer, and it turned out to be a treat.

They arrived wearing the kind of eccentric headgear that wouldn't look out of place at the Floral Dance and their intricate melodic harmonies held us spellbound all evening. They were also keen to encourage audience participation but, as they were new to us, we felt a little shy about joining in with their unfamiliar songs so they encouraged us by singing a verse then waiting for us to come in with the chorus.

But the Colombines had such high, clear, fluting voices, what if we couldn't match their key? This is where the title of this book comes in as their solution to our difficulty was simply not to worry unduly about our musical shortcomings, we could come in at random in any key we liked. Which we did, with gusto.

The song they had composed about the Harwich piano was called 'Silver Gilt Strings' and to demonstrate the sound of the dying piano as it sank beneath the waves, the lady playing the steel guitar struck a note that sounded off-key and somehow muffled.

It was a sad and plaintive song and it has haunted me ever since.

I only wish I had been there at the arts festival to enjoy the sight and sound of a lonely piano, defiant and proud, as she disappeared into the sea.

Sing along now if you know it...

She stands on the edge of the water
Where the waves roll just out of reach
And she laughs when they tell her she
shouldn't be there on the beach.
As the kids throw stones in the water
She laughs and she smiles and she sings.
As the pebbles they throw play a tune
on her silver gilt strings.
And it's 'Hey Mama rock, Mama rock
Mama roll, Mama rock Mama rock
Mama roll.'
Repeat
And she laughs, and she sings

And she plays on her silver gilt strings
Hey Mama rock, Mama roll Mama rock
Mama roll, Mama roll, Mama roll.
She stands with her feet in the water
Just watching the waves rise and fall
And she laughs when they tell her she shouldn't be there at all.
As the kids throw stones in the water
She laughs and she smiles and says, 'Bless.'
When they ask if her name is Joanna she tells them 'Good guess.'
It's hey Mama rock, Mama roll, Mama rock
Mama roll, Mama rock, Mama roll
Repeat
Now she stands shoulder deep in the water
With the waves crashing over her head
And she laughs when they say she should be in the parlour instead.
As the kids throw stones in the water

She says, 'Can't you just let me be?'
'I don't care what you say, I'm Joanna
The Queen of the Sea.'
It's hey Mama rock, Mama roll, Mama rock
Mama roll, Mama roll, Mama roll
Repeat
And she laughs, and she sings, and she plays on her silver gilt strings.
Hey Mama rock, Mama roll, Mama rock
Mama roll, Mama roll, Mama roll.

Sunshine and Sadness

This June has been a very long hot unsettling month. In fact the last couple of months I would quite happily rewind and undo, although where would you want to stop the rewind button - pre-Brexit? (oh, please let it be fake news). Pre-Trump? Surely, we all must have dreamt that one.

Certainly, pre the damn stupid waste of time and money which was the June 8th election.

End of political rant, with apologies to Brexiteers, peculiar American voters and friends of Theresa May.

I suppose the date I would most like to rewind past though is 16th June 2016, the day the Labour MP for Batley and Spen in West Yorkshire, Jo Cox, was murdered by a coward called Thomas Mair because she was a supporter of the European Union and immigration.

Mair considered that this made her a traitor to white people in Britain and therefore entitled him to take away her life.

On the anniversary of her murder this year, many events were held around the country to celebrate her truly exceptional life and to demonstrate that we have, in Jo's own words, 'more in common than that which divides us'.

If ever we needed to come together to support and comfort one another it is at this terrible time when we seem to wake up every day to a fresh disaster. On

March 22^{nd,} there was an attack on Westminster Bridge where innocent people were deliberately run down and killed or injured and a policeman, bravely trying to protect people, was stabbed to death.

On May 22nd at the Manchester Arena, a terrorists' bomb killed or injured hundreds of people who just wanted to enjoy a pop concert.

Then on June 14th, a tower block in London was engulfed in flames and many people lost their lives, all of this shown in terrifying pictures on our TV screens.

These tragic events seemed unreal against the background of beautiful blue summer skies as temperatures soared to record levels. The birds sang, here in

Suffolk wild poppies appeared everywhere, and the beautiful English countryside shone in contrast to the ugliness appearing nightly on our screens.

June and July are my favourite months. I love the long, light evenings. Welcome warmth after a long dark winter lifts my mood and seems to free my spirit.

My son, Alister, was born in June, his birthday coinciding with Father's Day giving us an excuse for a rare family get-together but we were unable to find a day when we were all free this year so instead Pete and I decided to go along to the Blaxhall Ship on our own.

Perhaps we would be lucky enough to recapture some of the joy of our first Blaxhall Folk weekend when we moved here in 2013, the unforgettable event that was the inspiration for my book about our move to Suffolk, *Harmonicas Round my Hat*. However, the atmosphere seemed different this year; even though the weather was as glorious as on that occasion the mood was far from one of noisy celebration.

The temperature when we arrived must have been in the mid-thirties and the punters outside had pushed their seats against the walls to take advantage of the few remaining inches of shade.

Dogs slept, panting, under the tables. Each person had their hands wrapped tightly around frosted beers and sunglasses and hats protected tender skin from the burning light that ate into the shrivelling patch of shade.

Sweaty musicians were pressed against the remaining wall, holding precious instruments out of the hammering heat. It was time to go inside.

The Blaxhall Ship music bar is not a large space, nor could it be called airy. Even with all the doors and windows propped open, air will not circulate. This is a snug built for huddling against the cold of winter, not a shelter from our current blowtorch summer.

Once inside, we realised there were far more people than chairs, so we decided on the novel formula of seating ourselves according to size (of person, not of chair)

This would make a great party game, and it was certainly an ice-breaker, although that day any ice would have melted long before it had a chance to break!

I took up my position with the doll-sized people along the back wall next to the door, keeping my poor, pink toes as far as I could from the blast furnace bouncing off the flagstones outside.

Our compere asked for volunteers to step up and perform but when asked I confessed that people would be willing to pay large sums of money for me to keep quiet, so they wisely passed me by.

Many, however, had brought along cherished musical instruments to entertain us, and very talented these people were too.

But it was a rather subdued event, the songs sung softly and with a sad quality that seemed to fit the new national mood of sorrow and regret.

I watched the faces of the audience during the performances; many looked close to tears.

Several people were holding hands or had their arms around their neighbours, it felt as if we needed to physically touch someone for comfort that day, despite the heat and lack of air.

No-one moved their chairs or fidgeted with their drinks, we just swayed gently to the music, together.

Doris and the Desperadoes

Our favourite singing barmaid, Doris from the Blaxhall Ship, has recently branched out into new territory by forming her own band of renegades collected from the towns and villages surrounding that great musical metropolis known as Leiston.

Unfortunately, she couldn't sign up Brad Pitt or Jonny Depp but I think they are getting a bit passé anyway. Not cutting edge enough for Leiston, not desperate enough to be Desperadoes. Well, not up to Doris' standards anyway.

Stormy Doris
&
The Desperado's
Present

An Acoustic Afternoon

At

The Royal Standard

Join in or just join us for the fun!

Wednesday
2.00pm –5.00pm ON

I first found out about this event on Facebook – imagine my excitement when amongst the usual updates from my family and friends, complete with pictures of their lunches (such fun) the above notification appeared:

I am a big fan of Leiston. Some people deride the little town, saying unkind things like, 'There's nothing there.' (Have they not been to Shottisham?) or 'I've heard they have some kind of problems with YOUTHS'. Probably littering or wearing T-shirts bearing misspelt rude slogans. Be afraid, be slightly afraid.

However, I always seem to have fun on my visits.

I love the old cinema/theatre on the high street; you really should visit, there's nothing not to like.

It has recently been refurbished with the most decadent, glamorous 1930's style loos, all spotlights round the mirrors and scarlet paint on the walls. A pleasure to visit and so clean.

It also has comfortable chairs, a real breakaway move for a cinema. Oh, how I wish they would try this at the concert hall in Snape. People take their own cushions along to the concerts there. I have even seen the staff take pity on their poor patrons' aching bottoms and pass out cushions before a performance begins.

But back in lovely Leiston Theatre we can all sit back in comfort to enjoy the entertainments, which is why we regularly make the forty-mile round trip. It is always worth it.

They also put on pantos, some of them quite rude. Well, you've got to keep those dangerous youths off the streets and 'Throbbin' Hood' should do the trick. Last year we went to a musical extravaganza to celebrate my Halloween birthday by watching a band called Merry Hell.

It was a full house, people could be seen queuing up outside which added to the '60s vibe that Leiston seems to exude - all it needs is a coffee bar with a juke-box playing Tremeloes hits and we're all back in the day...

Anyway, back to Doris and the Desperadoes.

On previous visits to Leiston when we arrived a little early, we discovered a small, unassuming pub called the Royal Standard.

This place instantly took me back to Southend's much loved and missed Hole in the Wall seafront pub to which my delightful Dad introduced me when I was about three years old. I would wander from table to table finishing the dregs of peoples' beers, they found this amusing.

Well, it doesn't seem to have done me any harm and it may go some way to explaining my strange obsession with pubs and the behaviour of their clientele.

The Royal Standard keeps all its more up-market furnishings for front-of-house, in the back it is a different story and this was where Doris and her friends were to be found.

The room was dominated by a pool table on which stood two large plates of sandwiches and sausage rolls - this boded well. Outside the wind howled and the rain tipped it down in the true British beach holiday tradition (it was August, remember). So we all huddled together round the bar with our assorted instruments and watched as the party took off.

Doris played her guitar and led the singing 'You picked a fine time to leave me, Lucille', complete with Mexican waving, was a particular highlight, and then the fun really began when she shouted out, 'We will now go round the room anti-clockwise'. German precision at its best.

There must have been around thirty people in that small room, perched on stools, propping up the bar, even sitting on the pool table (guarding the sandwiches?) and the only ones who didn't give a performance were Peter and myself. Shame on us!

We had Andy Ruffles, of Blaxhall Busk fame, on his fiddle with several other fiddlers who were new to us but obviously not to fiddling, a pair of lovely ladies who gave us 'Que sera, sera' (perfect for a pub sing along) plus storytellers; a man who told a long and complicated joke using a broad Suffolk accent that unfortunately prevents me from repeating it here, and a very quiet, nervous lady who recited poetry for us.

We listened respectfully to it all, feeling more and more ashamed of ourselves for our lack of contributions. There must be something we could bring to the party, in fact we have resolved to learn a few tunes by the next meeting of the Desperadoes, which seemed reassuringly far away in September, but it will surely come around all too quickly and there will be no-where to hide.

Doris will find us when she goes around the room anti-clockwise, and when that time comes I will be sure to let you know how we get on.

I may, however, be writing it from another part of the county, or even another country altogether. Que sera, sera.

Folk at the Froize

When we first moved to Suffolk in 2013, I made a list of aspirational places to visit and, being me, most of these places sold food and drink.

Also, they had to be a bit out of my league from the point of view of ambience and dress code, as I find I like a bit of a challenge when it comes to lists. That's the point of them-otherwise you might as well write out a shopping list with baked beans and toilet rolls on it.

We asked around our foodie friends in the village for suggestions of good places to splash the cash and increase our waistlines, and the name that seemed to come up most was a place in Chillesford called the Froize. This establishment certainly seemed to fit the list criteria in that it both looked fairly posh and was difficult to find.

It is a matter of great pride to me the way we have branched out in east Suffolk from our little village of Hollesley to the tiny outlying villages around Snape and Aldeburgh which can only be reached with great care along sand-strewn tracks haunted by giant tractors and misguided delivery drivers from the big supermarkets who seem to think they are still on the A12 looking at the speed at which they drive.

We are always in the car; Benhall, Aldringham, Thorpeness, Sweffling. If it's a dot on the map, we will find it if there is the promise of live music on offer. Which brings me back to Chillesford and the Froize.

Chillesford is on the lovely road to Snape where woodland walks beckon enticingly from the side of the road and in spring, bluebells carpet the way. Look it up on your paper satnav before you set out, however, if you are a stranger to these parts as we have heard terrifying tales of people being misled by the electronic version and ending up in other villages, thus turning up eventually at the Froize confused and late for lunch. Now you wouldn't want that to happen, would you?

We first encountered the legendary Froize hospitality through friends on the boules circuit who informed us that the owner, David Grimwood, was holding a rather special bash for his 60th birthday which he had called Davestock. How could we resist?

The great day, 5th October 2014, was sunny and crisp when we arrived and by the time the festivities kicked off in the evening, we had a magical bright moon to light our way. Marquees with fairy lights had been erected and as the temperature dropped, more and more people squeezed inside to perch on straw bales to enjoy the entertainment and the wonderful food being served from Gloria, the Froize's famous travelling food van.

We were treated to a musical hoe-down with much joyous dancing then Stephen Bayfield, father of Mat of 'walk and talk' fame, entertained us with his Suffolk brand of comedy and storytelling late into the night. This was when we realised that the Froize wasn't just a restaurant on a list, we had found ourselves a spiritual home.

Three years on and we now count ourselves as honorary members of the

Froize family. It is not posh, or scary, or out-of-reach as we had imagined when we first saw the rather grand exterior. It feels like a home from home, somewhere we can call in on our way to or from a walk along Butley Creek for soft drinks or a cheeky glass of red on a cold day.

We discovered the Butley Creek walk during a charity fundraiser. About forty of us hardy souls, many accompanied by their very excited dogs, turned up for the event and we lingered long at the restaurant door, held by the delicious smells wafting from within and the promise of lovely baked goods to come when we had finished our walk, generously provided for us by David.

The dogs sniffed each other out while excitedly getting their leads entangled as dogs invariably do. There is a gap in the market here, the no-tangle lead, a money-spinner if ever there was one.

The humans just discussed the weather prospects (iffy), and the possible condition of the footpaths we were about to traverse (boggy, worthy of wellies) with characteristic hikers' glee. We didn't want blue skies and well-tended pathways. We wanted a struggle, we wanted to get our boots muddy and feel that we had earned our reward.
We were **proper walkers.** Some of us even had sticks!

It didn't rain in the end and the paths were fine, no one fell over or got lost and the dogs behaved themselves too.

We also raised lots of money for the Brain Tumour Charity, so it was altogether a grand day out, and we had earned our cake.

And what cakes they were — a feast from the Froize, all home-made of course including the best mincemeat I had ever tasted, and I am famous for my mince pies. Unlimited coffee too. Life doesn't get much better than that. But I digress - what of the Folk?

Well, it took a long time for us to actually get round to attending a Folk night at the Froize and I am rather ashamed to admit that the reason was entirely mercenary.

We are not used to paying to see bands perform. For years we had grown used to just rocking up at pubs and other venues to be treated to brilliant music from creative people who wrote their own songs and played their own instruments for however much we felt like dropping into the hat.

Often there was no hat so we would enjoy all this bounty for free, and we had come to feel that somehow this was ok, that we were entitled to free entertainment just because we had bothered to turn up, but really it isn't ok at all. People deserve to get paid for their work and these were talented individuals who were performing for our enjoyment. We sometimes bought their CDs as if we were doing them a favour – shame on us.

But the good people at the Froize, bless them, charge a decent amount (around £15) for a musical evening, with tapas, and it took quite a while for us to warm to this concept. We had been missing a treat.

We finally took the plunge in May 2017 and made the trip out to Chillesford to see an Indie folk duo called the Worry Dolls. These two girls hail from London but their music reflects American folk as they have recorded much of their material in Nashville. Their harmonies were sublime and they peppered their songs with a fresh and gentle humour that had us all warming to them from the start.

After about an hour we had a break for food, laid out by the Froize food fairies on tables in the bar for us to help ourselves, which we did with huge Suffolk enthusiasm. Then it was a quick refill of our glasses and back for more music.

The sound quality was truly amazing, due to the expert engineering of Jon

Hart from Honey and the Bear - you would have thought you were in a top music venue not a small country restaurant and all for £15 per head, what had been holding us back for so long?

We have since been along twice for more magical musical events and are planning several more, but my favourite experience so far has been the al fresco experience of 27th August when we were treated to the talents of a Scottish quartet called Tannara.

August 2017 was not the Mediterranean experience we had hoped for after the record breaking hot spell of early spring. In fact it was COLD!

We should have taken blankets with us- other people did, along with scarves, woolly hats and fluffy socks (I was wearing flip-flops, I never learn).

David had lit the bonfire so we bagged a place nearest the flames and refused to budge all night despite our neighbours' attempts to infiltrate. We took it in turns to queue for food to protect our privileged fireside position. Next time we will bring duvets. And onesies.

But it was worth all the discomfort- Tannara were amazing, they played jigs and old folk ballads and accompanied their music with stories and jokes that warmed even my frozen toes.

The entertainment continued late into the night, with dancing and audience participation galore. In fact, we enjoyed it so much we didn't want it to end so we clapped wildly and stamped our feet (I couldn't feel mine by now so I just whooped a bit, very embarrassing) and the band agreed to play another song but only if they could come down off the stage and share with us the warmth of the fire.

We all moved respectfully back so that Tannara could gather round with their instruments. These included a beautiful and no doubt very expensive harp which the band manoeuvred carefully into place and then - well, honestly this was a magical moment to treasure. It felt like a religious experience to be gathered in the dark around the dancing flames as these four people stood with us pouring out their gorgeous songs.

I can't remember what they played but the way it made me feel will stay with me for a long, long time.

Lights - Cameras - Earplugs

It had to happen. It was all our own fault. We should have known better, but a promise is a promise, too many people had been present at the last open mic for the Desperadoes, and a Doris never forgets.

This is how Peter and I ended up performing, in public, at not one but two venues, on the SAME DAY! We didn't want to. We really, really didn't want to. But short of moving back to Essex or going around in disguise, there was no way out.

Doris was going around the room anti-clockwise and she had us in her sights.
It wasn't as if we lacked practise. If we hadn't lived in a detached house our activities would have been reported to the noise abatement crew long ago, as Pete plinked away on the ukulele and I struggled to find a key I could stay in without doing some damage to my vocal chords or the windows.

I came in at random in any key I liked, and the lyrics I sang were pretty random too.

It occurred to me that if Pete and I formed a duo we could call ourselves 'Cognative Dissonance'. At least it would give the audience something to smile about until they heard us play.

On September 6th, a grey and blustery afternoon when Leiston didn't look its best and even the scary youths were in hiding, we sidled into the back room of the Royal Standard, looking shifty and trying not to let people notice that we came armed with a ukulele. This isn't easy...

Everyone seemed in a mellow frame of mind, but then the bar had been open for a fair while.

I settled down with a large glass of red (poor Pete was driving so he settled for a slimline tonic and fortified himself with some cheese and tomato sandwiches from the pool table buffet). We found a space in the corner of the room on a large squashy sofa next to our old boules buddy, Bluesy Ray Booth, who had also brought his uke. He warmed the audience up nicely, and then it was our turn.

We had decided to begin with something simple, 'Colours' by Donovan.

Hopefully everyone would know this popular old favourite (?) and help us out by singing along, but no. Either no-one else had ever heard of 'Colours' or our audience were so keen to hear the performance they were keeping quiet in order to savour every word.

Big mistake.

I couldn't remember the words, well not in the right order anyway.
Heaven knows, 'Colours' is not a

complicated song. It only has about five short verses and these are conveniently themed around the colour being celebrated; green, blue and yellow in fact, although I think yellow may have been mentioned twice. I certainly mentioned it twice, but by then I couldn't have told you what I was singing about.

I was just glad we hadn't attempted anything by Bob Dylan. Can you imagine what we could have done with 'Sad Eyed Lady of the Lowlands'? Eleven and a half minutes of opportunities for misheard lyrics and cognitive dissonance, mmm...

Is it just me or does everyone who sings hear a six-year old cockney performing in their head? Like Lena Zavaroni, but without the cute hair?

And why is it so hard to breathe and sing at the same time. I'm sure Kiri Te Kanawa never had these problems.

At last we came to the end of the song - everyone clapped politely (but quietly, they didn't want to encourage us too much or we might want to give them another song) and Pete slipped his uke back into the case, pushing it firmly under the couch. They weren't getting an encore out of us, no matter how much they begged.

You would think that was enough suffering for one day, but no, we were on a roll.

That evening was the festival of madness that was Horse Clarke's Old School Blow Out at the good old Sweffling White Horse.

There would be vinyl and audience participation galore, and again we had promised to perform. Pete has a regular spot as kazoo soloist, but tonight we were to be upgraded to a duo, Pete and Sue unveiled, for one night only (definitely).

Undeterred by our disaster at the Royal Standard, we had decided to murder 'Colours' again. Well, we knew how it went by now, didn't we?

The White Horse crowd were old music buffs, so they were sure to know the words and could help drown us out, I mean sing along...

We really should have printed the words out and taken them along, as if anything this performance was worse than the last. I had never heard a deathly hush in the White Horse before, the only sound being my terrified squeaks.

I'm sure I only sang one verse but repeated it three times. Why didn't anyone stop me? I thought these people were my friends.

Undeterred, we pressed on with the next song in our repertoire, that trusty pub favourite 'San Francisco Bay Blues'.

This was more like it, and this time we tried a tactic that hopefully disguised our lack of musical talent and inability to agree on the order of the lyrics, we simply played faster and faster.

In fact, we sounded like that part of the last night of the Proms, you know the bit, where the audience and the orchestra get into a race to see who can get to the end of the piece first. Except in our case the audience didn't join in, they left us to it as we galloped to a merciful conclusion.

This time when we finished people just looked down into their glasses and mumbled something about refills. If ever alcohol was needed, it was now.

This experience came back to me recently at the White Horse when a band had an unfortunate encounter with word loss (they gave up after two verses, now why didn't we think of that) and then turned to the audience and asked, 'shall we play something we know?' I only wish we'd tried this novel approach ourselves. The one good thing to come out of this nightmare is that people have stopped asking me to sing.

Pete can carry on playing his kazoo solos and retuning all the ukes scattered around the White Horse.

This is our new role in life, ukulele tuner to the stars and silent partner/kazoo minder.

Sixth September 2017 - a day and a night to forget.

Exotic Visitors

We had become very familiar with seeing our favourite local acts and following them loyally to far flung places such as Beccles and Halesworth but sometimes we encountered unexpected treats in the form of – foreign visitors.

A very welcome example of this musical diversity occurred one September night at the Blaxhall Busk.

There we sat huddled up in our usual corner, munching crisps and debating whether or not to indulge in another glass of red (it had been a heavy week) when our eyes were caught by a strange and rather unsettling phenomenon, a New Performer. This person was quite arresting to look at, filling a lot more space than your average Suffolk specimen (in a good way) and oozing with stage presence to go with his size.

He somehow looked strangely familiar, and we put our heads together to work out how this could be as not only was he a newcomer to the busk, he was also a newcomer to the UK. In fact, he was — wait for it — American.

We then decided the familiarity came from his close personal resemblance to a character from the Harry Potter films, and there followed one of those conversations, I'm sure you know the ones, where each member of the group shouts out a different name.

'Hagrid!'
No, Hagrid is too young.
'Ron Weasley's Dad.'
Ditto, and our man doesn't have ginger hair.
'Voldemort!'
You definitely need to cut back on the beers.
'Harry's uncle.'

Of course, that's the one, Harry's uncle whatsisname – what is his name, Geoffrey, David, Richard – no, no, it'll come to me in a minute. Oh, the frustration and scratching of heads as we groped desperately for the name, but it continued to elude us until Susie introduced the mystery man as Vernon Northover. Of course ...

Uncle Vernon Dursley, as played so brilliantly by the late, great Richard Griffiths. Not only was this guy the very image of Uncle Vernon, but he was called Vernon as well!

We were overcome by this amazing coincidence, which just goes to show that as a group we should drink more tonic water. Without the gin.

It turned out that Uncle Vernon was a consummate performer, a genuine crowd-pleaser with a rich chocolatey voice and a feel for the blues that reminded me of Eric Burdon of the Animals, with whom I was briefly and unrequitedly in love in my teens.

Vernon played on for a large part of the evening, and my favourite was in fact originally by the Animals.

Vernon: 'I'm just a soul whose intentions are good.'

Audience: 'Oh Lord, please don't let me be misunderstood.'

The old walls shook and our eardrums were blasted, but Vernon played on.

'We gotta get out of this place. If it's the last thing we ever do...'

Honestly, it was like having Eric in the room with us in the form of a huge, grizzled Yank with a blues guitar. And then to round off the perfect night Vernon informed us that before he returned to the States he would be at the Angel in Woodbridge the following evening performing his complete set in the famous Gin Room.

Would we like to go? Of course we would.

We don't often venture into Woodbridge in the evening, put off by the uncertainty of parking and fear of large aggressive crowds looking for pizza and McDonald's (they'd be lucky). We tend to stick to smaller, more intimate venues where we know lots of people and there is the chance of free food.

However, the Angel has the wonderful advantage of holding an enormous stock of differently flavoured gins and beautiful they were to behold. They weren't cheap, but boy were they cheerful.

We each had a pink peppercorn gin which came in a large balloon glass which looked as if it held half a pint.

They were delicious but we found the peppercorns rather intrusive and had to request straws to avoid them, although one or two of the little blighters still managed to startle us by making it up the straws when we weren't looking. This certainly helped to spice up our taste buds.

It must have also tickled the taste buds of the group at the table next to us, who had tried so many different gins there was barely room for another balloon glass on the table. They certainly seemed to be having a nice time: even at 10pm when one of their party optimistically suggested getting something to eat and was met by gasps of amazement from the rest of us. Food? In Woodbridge? At 10pm?
What outlandish part of the British Isles did these people hail from?

In the end they settled for a few packets of crisps and another selection of artisan gins. Who needs food?

Vernon and his pals were nicely warmed up by now too, and Vernon announced that it was time for him to get his toys out. What could he mean? We'd heard rumours about what Americans get up to after a few beers (dressing up as Donald Trump complete with orange wigs, trying to convert random people to Christianity, marrying their horses) but sharing their toys?

We weren't to be kept in the dark for long though – Vernon reached into his travelling case and brought out several large tambourines and a handsome set of cowbells which he passed out to eager fans and then the real fun began.

We got songs by Cream, the Animals, the Yardbirds and of course the Eagles: 'One of these Nights', 'Heartache Tonight', 'Peaceful Easy Feelin' – we bashed our tambourines and waggled our cowbells with gusto, those of us that weren't dancing like dervishes that is.

The gin room at the Angel is far from spacious, especially as most of it was taken up by Vernon and his companions, but we made the most of every inch. Oh, what a night, as the Four Seasons might have said.

We were very sad when the evening ended and lovely Vernon departed for the Land of the Free. We eagerly await his next visit to our shores.

From America to Canada now and a lively duo called April Moon who originally hailed from Saskatchewan but have been living in the UK since 2012, appearing in exotic places such as Liverpool, Blackpool, Preston and Manchester.

April Moon comprise Jaime April and Jason Moon (what a fabulous combination of names that is, like something out of Woodstock. You would expect Bob Dylan and Joanie Mitchell to give their children such names if they had ever got together) and the first thing we noticed about them was how LOUD they were.

Apart from Vernon the music at the Ship tends towards the quiet and introspective, so this rock and roll approach was a bit of a shock. It took us a while to appreciate this change of culture but once our ears had adjusted we found ourselves cheering and clapping like a crowd of One Direction fans.

I'm always up for a new experience and feeling the old Ship floorboards vibrating beneath my feet was certainly one of those.

Jaime and Jason performed their own songs along with a few well-known crowd pleasers thrown in to keep us happy, and do you know the louder they played the better they sounded. Go Canada (sounds more exciting than Go Preston).

Unfortunately, our friends had to get back to Essex so we were forced to leave while April Moon were still rocking. Pete apologised for this outrage and explained that it wasn't that we didn't like their music, and they took our departure in good part I'm pleased to say. Don't want the Canadians taking agin* us, especially ones with Northern connections – scary place Preston.

*Agin is the Irish version of 'Against'.

Peaceful Easy Feelings
Christmas 2017

We have now reached the stage in our Suffolk musical adventuring where we find ourselves recognised by band members instead of the other way around. This is largely because of Pete's habit of offering to tune in guitars or ukuleles for people, whether they want him to or not.

Also, he likes to share. This means that on Old School Blow Out nights (they are known as OSBOs, and we have the stickers to prove it. And we wear them!), Pete takes along his trusty kazoo, the uke, a bongo drum plus a drumstick he fashioned for himself using a twig and masking tape, and a triangle originally bought for me which he has added to his percussive collection.

Pete then spends the evening passing his various instruments around and getting into discussions with the musicians. At least it stops him singing.

Anyway, we now find on our nights out vaguely familiar-looking people will approach to ask if we are coming to see them play in various remote parts of Suffolk. Happy to oblige, folks, happy to oblige.

In a new form of audience participation, we have started to collect our own musicians from our usual haunts and pass them round to other venues who might appreciate our discoveries.

The first of these exciting new finds appeared at Blaxhall one Thursday. His name is Finn and he hails from the wilds of Rendlesham but we won't hold that against him. I took to him even before he began to play as he bears a resemblance to my son Alister, also a keen guitar enthusiast.

Alister used to write his own songs as a teenager and play them to me in his bedroom. I cherish these memories, as I am sure most mothers would agree that their own offspring outshine Prince and Jimmy Hendrix any day. My own mother didn't share this opinion however, as when Alister played one of his songs for her she uttered the immortal words 'You're not very good, are you?'...

This has gone into family history and we still laugh about it twenty years on, but I don't think Alister has forgiven her.

Anyway, back to the lovely Finn from Rendlesham. He has many virtues apart from being an Alister Thompson look-alike: he writes a lot of his own material, dark miserable songs about the trials of a troubled life and the general desperation of the human condition. Right up my street, can't stand all that happy clappy Pharrell Williams type rubbish. This is folk music, it's meant to make you want to slit your wrists.

I recently heard a singer-songwriter say that when she was stuck for something to write about she fell back on the basic folk fodder of sending Johnnie off to sea and then drowning him. Good tip.

Then, just when I thought the evening couldn't get any better, Finn apologised for playing a cover and launched into 'Counting Stars' by One Republic. The crowd at Blaxhall don't normally show too much respect to newcomers, but even they put down their glasses, stopped talking and paid attention.

He was amazing, we stood up and cheered and clapped, it was quite a moment I can tell you.

Afterwards we went up to Finn and told him how much we had enjoyed hearing him play and asked if he had ever been to the White Horse in Sweffling. Seems he hadn't, so we told him all about the OSBO nights in the hope that he would come along and to our delight the next time we were there we found Finn perched on one of the high chairs happily chatting to the other musicians.

Pete and I were thrilled to show off our new discovery and the OSBO crowd welcomed Finn with open arms so I suppose we can now consider ourselves impresarios and I look forward to a little entourage of musicians to promote, for a fee of course. We'll make our fortune here in Suffolk yet.

As a complete contrast to the usual doom-laden fare we know and love so much, I would like to share with you a delightful moment from the Thursday busk at Blaxhall involving a father and son partnership charmingly known as 'Keep up Dad'.

This duo consists of Roger Miles and

his son Freddie who often entertain us with their brilliant guitar playing but on this occasion it was more of the old style comedy double act to light up my evening.

Think Morecombe and Wise singing 'Will You Miss Me Tonight when I'm Gone?' with Eric singing the main part while Ernie and his band in the background provide the musical accompaniment of 'Boom, ooh, ya-ta-ta-taaaa'. For some reason the sheer daftness of this always has me in hysterics, which is probably why I enjoyed Roger and Freddie's unintentional version using the lovely 1950's Jim Reeves classic 'He'll Have to Go' so much.

But Keep up Dad played it as a long running family argument thus-

Roger: 'Put your sweet lips a little closer to the phone.'

Freddie: 'It's in D, Dad.'

Roger: 'This is D.'

'Let's pretend that we're together all alone.'

Freddie: 'That's D flat.'

Roger: 'No it isn't.'

'I'll tell the man to turn the juke-box way down low.'

Stops, looking unsure for a moment, fiddles with guitar, looks slightly nervous but continues in D (flat?).

'And you can tell your friend there with you, he'll have to go.'

Personally, I would never perform with family, you just can't win.

Pete and I had resolved to make the Christmas of 2017 as joyous an occasion as possible. We have much to be thankful for, this has been an exceptional year in many ways and one of the best things to happen occurred back in January when we joined with our good friend Mat Bayfield to walk each day in different areas around our towns and villages to raise money for the Brain Tumour Charity, the one referred to in my chapter about the Froize.

Our little band became known as the 'Walkie Talkies', as this is what we did, apart from eating cake.

Pete and I gained much support (and weight) from this and made many good friends as a result. This is also how we came to discover the White Horse so that must be how karma works.

The pub now hosts a charity walk on the first Sunday of every month and these are often themed so we have enjoyed foraging for wild food and also for Christmas decoration foliage so that our front door this year was enhanced by the beautiful leaves and berries taken from a chilly Sweffling march.

I also borrowed a guide to mushroom gathering from the library and ended up with a tempting (and somewhat terrifying) basket of goodies to cook up for my nervous man. Would we need the air ambulance on standby once more?

As it turned out, I only dared to cook the parasol mushrooms which really are simple to identify and delicious to eat.

They grow prolifically in the sandy soil of the Hollesley heath lands and reach a huge size, providing a hearty addition to stews and curries in our kitchen. I feel a cook book coming on.

The charity walks started with a three-mile stroll around the lonely windswept beach that is called Shingle Street, just two miles from our home.

The other walkers relied on us to lead them, as they were unfamiliar with the area, and I was so proud to see Pete, who struggles with walking due to arthritis and knee problems, walking at the head of our little group with Mat, who of course has struggles of his own.

We continued with these walks as winter warmed into spring, but on a walk in Tunstall forest to celebrate Mat's birthday in May we noticed that Mat himself was tiring and having difficulty completing the walk. From then on, his condition worsened until in August, when he sang with the Broadside Boys at the FolkEast Festival at Glemham

Hall, he needed to use a wheelchair to get around.

We have now learned that his brain tumour has grown again causing nerve damage and paralysis so at this moment Mat is undergoing chemotherapy in an attempt to shrink his tumour. He remains cheerful and lives his life to the full, in fact in January he and his lovely Kelly are getting married.

The walks continue without him and to date they have raised well over £20,000 for the charity for which Mat recently won a much deserved Unsung Hero award, which as he said has a certain irony considering he is a singer.

We have a long list of musical ambitions for 2018 and an idea was presented to us when we attended the December Folk at the Froize concert featuring Ange

Hardy, a singer songwriter from Somerset.

Ange is also a keen supporter of new musical talent and she has devised a system to publicise bands by taking photos of yourself at a gig holding up a little origami fox and posting them on social media. She supplies the sheet with instructions on how to fold it into the fox but we cheated and obtained one someone had made earlier at the Froize. Making origami animals is one of the many talents I have yet to master.

Now we can go forth into the new year armed with our folded friend and show our love of the local talent to the world at large.

We plan to find new venues and bands, perhaps branching out into types of music we have yet to appreciate. It is too easy to stay in your comfort zone with the people and places you have come to know and love, forgetting that only a year ago you had no idea this stuff existed.

I have been inspired by Mat and Kelly to try something challenging next year.

In March, they took a holiday in New York and visited the jazz clubs of Harlem, where, in a small basement club unfrequented by tourists and where theirs were the only white faces in the room, they were made welcome and Kelly got to sing with Maxine Brown.

I often think of how this must have made Kelly feel, a true life-changing experience gained by overcoming your fears.

I felt a huge sense of achievement when I became an author for the first time at the age of sixty seven, after four years of struggling with the terrors of technology, so I am sure something else is waiting out there for me next year. All I need to do is grab hold of it and not worry about making a fool of myself.

Friends and family have suggested Parkrun, and this sounds quite a good idea as many of the park runners are rumoured to be even older than me and it would be a good excuse to buy new trainers and some colourful lycra outfits. Or borrow Pete's jogging bottoms until I shift the Christmas bulges.

One thing is for sure though, it won't involve singing. Been there, done that, better leave it to those with talent. Suffolk certainly has plenty of that and I look forward to many more happy musical discoveries in the pubs and restaurants of my beloved county.

Use it or Lose it

When we bought our Suffolk home in June 2012, we used to commute from Essex to our new village hideaway in Hollesley as we were house-sitting for our daughter while she and her family spent time in Singapore where her husband was working.

We ourselves continued with our jobs as school bus driver and passenger assistant for disabled children on Canvey Island, a very stressful occupation due to the horrendous traffic in that part of Essex, and we would regularly escape to the quiet lanes of Hollesley on a Friday night, celebrating our arrival with a pint and some fish and chips in the Shepherd and Dog.

It felt as if we had a little holiday home, but we became tired of the horrible journey down the A12 so on February 20th 2013 we packed our remaining belongings into suitcases and made the move properly.

I still remember fondly the excitement of waking up the next morning knowing we were home for good. I felt like a child on Christmas day.

We spent our first year as permanent Suffolk residents checking out the local pubs and eateries but there was one establishment that unfortunately we thought we would have to relegate to the happy memory category; the lovely Butley Oyster pub which had stood deep in the countryside about a five-mile drive from our new home.

We visited the Oyster to celebrate my birthday on 31st October 2012 (this was during one of our half-term escape visits) and enjoyed a delicious but rather quiet dinner. We were the only customers, even the bar was empty so considering the date it all felt a little spooky.

The next day the Oyster shut its doors for the last time and did not reopen for more than four years.

We would pass the sad empty building on our way to play boules in Aldringham on Thursdays and ponder on the future of the Butley Oyster.

Work was being carried out intermittently and we heard rumours that permission was being sought to convert the building into holiday cottages.

Now the definition of a village is a collection of houses with a public meeting place, be it a shop, pub or village hall. Without one of these amenities the area is just a hamlet, a scattering of lonely houses with no real purpose.

Those places tend to have no public transport and become just dormitories for people with cars who work and shop elsewhere and so have no real connection with their neighbours. No heart, no soul, just sad really.

Then in 2016, we started to hear rumours that plans were afoot to resurrect the Butley Oyster as a pub, with the brave new owners refurbishing the rather tired old building giving it a cinema, a shop and a micro-brewery.

We were very excited and followed the developments with a close interest as we drove past on Thursdays peering at the work in progress as we went.

The big day dawned on 19th March 2017 when we inspected the smart newly opened pub. The refurbishment had kept the best features of the old pub with the beams and windows left intact but posh new toilets and tasteful wallpaper bringing the place into the 21st century.

We were impressed, especially when we learnt that the Oyster was going to revive the popular folk music nights.

Butley used to be on the circuit for musicians who also played at the Crown in Snape and the good old Blaxhall Ship, so we knew we would be in for a treat.
I am happy to report that nearly one year on the pub is thriving and it is such a pleasure to see it being used by locals as well as ramblers and holidaymakers. The village has a heart again.

A similar story surrounds our favourite pub, the famed White Horse in Sweffling. In 2003 it closed and the plan was to convert it to a house but Suffolk

County Council and the people from the Campaign for Real Ale take a dim view of this kind of behaviour and are active in preventing planning permission being given for the change of use if the pub is the only one in the village (hooray).

The new owners of the White Horse, Mark and Marie, have printed a very interesting book about the process of acquiring their pub. It is called The Story of the Pub with no Bar and sells in the pub with half the proceeds going to a local charity.

Mark and Marie came across an advertisement on the internet detailing the place as the former White Horse and as they were only interested in buying the attached land for a small campsite they made an appointment to see it.

They had expected to view a house but when they got inside they saw that the building had never been converted or lived in and even though all the pub furniture and even the bar had been removed, it still felt (and smelt) like a pub.

The estate agent seemed to think there would be no problem converting the building to a house, but when Mark and Marie spoke to Suffolk County Council later that same day they were told that it was a pub and would remain so until someone could prove it was not viable.

The upshot of a long and complicated story was the happy news that in the winter of 2011 Mark and Marie re-opened the White Horse as a pub, and the rest is history.

We went along at the winter solstice of 2017 to help celebrate the pub's sixth birthday, complete with a party along the lines of those held for six-year olds with cake, silly games and a puppet show (although this was rather adult, and great fun it was too). Pure White Horse mayhem and joy at the darkest time of the year.

I am telling the stories of these two very different ventures to illustrate the point that these sorts of places do not just happen overnight, they are not mere additions to a chain, each indistinguishable from the last, they are the result of huge amounts of time, hard work and financial bravery on the part of the owners, and they deserve our support.

I cannot imagine our lives without the musical evenings, the joyous get togethers, the walking and talking with friends old and new that have resulted from just exploring and finding places that warm our souls. In the cold, dark winter months they save our sanity, and in the summer, there is always someone to share the lovely Suffolk skies with us.

Sadly, we also see around us the results of local apathy, the closed pubs and ghost villages where the inhabitants might as well live in Belgium or Normandy for all the connection they have with the place they call home.

Are we strange in needing so much contact with our neighbouring villages? Is it so unusual now to be content just to sit in a pub with a pie and a pint and join in the local gossip?

But one thing I'm sure of, if we don't support these places one day they will be gone and something very precious will have passed with them. Use it or lose it.

Dear Reader

If you have enjoyed reading this book,
then please tell your friends and relatives
and leave a review on Amazon.
Thank you.

About the Author

Sue Thompson moved with her husband to a small Suffolk village in 2013 and set about making a new life for herself, which she described in her first book "Harmonicas round my Hat". During this time she fell in love with the local folk music scene and also became a little too fond of audience participation. Now she can share her unique up- close and very personal experiences, some hilarious, some humiliating, but all sure to make you want to join in the fun.

https://www.facebook.com/Sue-Thompson-Author-1784360638472543/?pnref=story.unseen-section

Harmonicas Round my Hat

ISBN-13: 978-1545419021

Some of the many reviews on Amazon

"A well thought out and rather moving book capturing
village life in Suffolk. Looking forward to what the
author comes up with next..."

"Loved this book. Beautifully written with lovely
descriptions of the local area."

"What a lovely book! Beautifully written in an engaging,
happy and very witty style. Sue's descriptive writing
makes you feel like you're actually there with her -
on her rollercoaster adventure of moving to Suffolk
and making new friends. She has a wonderful way
of looking at life and I enjoyed every page. Looking
forward to the next one already!"

Printed in Poland
by Amazon Fulfillment
Poland Sp. z o.o., Wrocław

22659680R00081